HOMOSEXUALITY, THE BIBLE AND THE FUNDAMENTALIST TRADITION

A Reply to the Lambeth Conference

DAVID BRUCE TAYLOR

THE LESBIAN AND GAY
CHRISTIAN MOVEMENT

By the same author:
Mark's Gospel as Literature and History *(SCM Press)*
The Ten Commandments as the Foundation of Morality *(Minerva Press)*

© David Bruce Taylor 1999

ISBN 0 946310 08 4

First published in 1999 by:
Lesbian and Gay Christian Movement (LGCM)
Oxford House, Derbyshire Street, London E2 6HG
Tel / Fax: + 44 (0)207 739 1249
E-mail: lgcm@aol.com
Web: http://www.members.aol.com/lgcm
Counselling HELPLINE +44 (0)207 739 8134

The Lesbian and Gay Christian Movement is a registered charity No. 1048842

LGCM is a non-profit Company Limited by guarantee registered in England and Wales No. 3092197

Typeset, printed and bound by
Gwilym Jones & Son, Penrhyndeudraeth, Gwynedd

CONTENTS

Foreword by Prof. Adrian Thatcher 4

The Improper Use of Scripture 5

Homosexuality in the Old Testament 16

Homosexuality in the New Testament 26

Jesus and Liberation *versus* Paul and Constraint 39

Picking and Choosing 50

The Proper Use of Scripture 58

FOREWORD

The Lambeth Conference of Anglican Bishops (August 1998) rejected 'homosexual practice as incompatible with scripture' (Resolution 1.10(d). David Taylor's timely work will allow its readers to make up their minds for themselves about the truth of this part of the resolution. What does scripture actually say about homosexual practice? And once we have listed attentively to the teaching of scripture, how do we appropriate them for ourselves?

This book offers a cool, careful examination of biblical passages which are about homosexuality or are referred to in contemporary discussions of the subject. The tone throughout is cool and fair. While it sustains a 'non-fundamentalist' position consistently throughout, it is never polemical. The attitude of Jesus to the observance of the sabbath as it is expounded here provides a lasting picture of him as a compassionate and merciful interpreter of law. We see in Jesus confirmation that God requires mercy, not sacrifice. Fundamentalists get this requirement the wrong way round.

There are many insights in this book for gay Christians and everyone else who wants a serious but accessible treatment of biblical teaching on homosexuality. While Christians who are outside the 'fundamentalist tradition' will agree with the author about 'the improper use of scripture' in the first chapter, they may well disagree with this account of 'proper use of scripture' at the end of the book. The likelihood that the Bible is 'delusory' or 'illusory' yet still able to offer 'a message of hope' may seem to some to be itself delusory: others may find in this position a subtle contribution to the widespread debate about the how the Bible ought to be used. It is an informative and compelling read.

ADRIAN THATCHER
Professor of Applied Theology
The College of St Mark and St. John, Plymouth.

The Improper Use of Scripture

> At that time Jesus went through the grainfields on the sabbath; his disciples were hungry, and they began to pluck ears of grain and to eat. But when the Pharisees saw it, they said to him, "Look, your disciples are doing what is not lawful to do on the sabbath. " He said to them, "Have you not read what David did, when he was hungry, and those who were with him: how he entered the house of God and ate the bread of the Presence, which it was not lawful for him to eat nor for those who were with him, but only for the priests? Or have you not read in the law how on the sabbath the priests in the temple profane the sabbath, and are guiltless? I tell you something greater than the temple is here. And if you had know what this means, 'I desire mercy, and not sacrifice', you would not have condemned the guiltless. For the Son of man is lord of the sabbath." (Matthew 12:1-8)

The occasion of this book is the resolution by the 1998 Lambeth Conference that homosexuality is incompatible with any genuine form of Christian religion, the reason being that it is unambiguously condemned by the Scriptures of both the Old and New Testaments. It is certainly true that there are passages in both testaments which condemn it, though equally it is misleading to claim (as members of the Conference did from time to time) that it is repeatedly or consistently condemned by the Scriptures. As we shall see, the Old Testament only very rarely mentions the subject at all (there are at most three unambiguous references), while in the New Testament, outside the writings of Paul, there is a single passage which probably refers to it. In fairness, not too much should be made of this rarity of utterance, since the likely cause of it is that the subject was considered unmentionable rather than in any way unimportant; but fairness equally demands that the rarity itself should be noted. The point I shall be making in this first chapter is that however much Scripture condemns it, if it can be shown (as I believe it can) that such a condemnation is both unnecessary and cruel, if it can be shown that the Fundamentalist tradition - like the pious, perhaps, in every age - is here demanding sacrifice and not mercy, then no amount of appeal to Scripture will justify it. For that is precisely the principle that Jesus is establishing above, in opposition to the religious authorities of his day who unquestionably had Scripture an their side.

If we want to know what the Bible of Jesus' day (which was essentially the same as our own Old Testament) has to say about sabbath observance, we cannot do better than start with the following:

> While the people of Israel were in the wilderness, they found a man gathering sticks on the sabbath day. And those who found him gathering sticks brought him to Moses and Aaron, and to all the congregation. They put him in custody because it had not been made plain what should be done to him. And the LORD said to Moses, "The man shall be put to death; all the congregation shall stone him with stones outside the camp." And all the congregation brought him outside the camp, and stoned him to death with stones, as the LORD commanded Moses. (Numbers 15:32-35)

The reason for Jesus' opposition to the sabbath regulations of his day appears to have been that they fulfilled no real moral purpose; they were therefore unnecessary, and could often be so pointlessly inconvenient as to be cruel. In all three synoptic gospels the story with which we began (Matthew 12:1-8, Mark 2:23-28, Luke 6:1-5) is immediately followed by the healing of the man the withered hand, which makes precisely this point. It also suggests that it was on this point of carelessness about sabbath observance that Jesus incurred the hostility of both the religious ('Pharisees') and the political ('Herodians' – not mentioned in Matthew) activists of his day.

As we can see from the excerpt above from Numbers, there can be no doubt that it was Jesus' opponents that had Scripture 'unambiguously' on their side. And they didn't simply have to rely on a passage which, even in Jesus' day, would have appeared archaicly severe. How could Jesus reply to anyone quoting the following:

> Thus said the LORD to me: "Go and stand in the Benjamin Gate, by which the kings of Judah enter and by which they go out, and in all the gates of Jerusalem, and say: ' Hear the word of the LORD, you kings of Judah, and all Judah, and all the inhabitants of Jerusalem, who enter by these gates. Thus says the LORD: Take heed for the sake of your lives, and do not bear a burden on the sabbath day or bring it in by the gates of Jerusalem. And do not carry a burden out of your houses on the sabbath or do any work, but keep the sabbath day holy, as I commanded your fathers. Yet they did not listen or incline their ear, but stiffened their neck, that they might not hear and receive instruction. But if you listen to me, says the LORD, and bring in no burden by the gates of this city on the sabbath day, but keep the sabbath day holy and do no work on it, then there shall enter by the gates of this city kings who sit on the throne of David, riding in chariots and on horses, they and their princes, the men of Judah and the inhabitants of Jerusalem; and this city shall be inhabited for ever. And people shall come from the cities of Judah and from the places round about Jerusalem, from the land of Benjamin, from the Shephelah, from the hill country, and from the Negeb, bringing burnt offerings and sacrifices, cereal offerings and frankincense, and bringing thank offerings to the house of the LORD. But if you do not listen to me, to keep the sabbath day holy, and not to bear a burden and enter by the gates of Jerusalem on the sabbath day, then I will kindle a fire in its gates, and it shall devour the palaces of Jerusalem and shall not be quenched.' "
>
> (Jeremiah 17:19-27)

If Jesus thought that the sabbath regulations served no useful or moral purpose, he had to face the fact that he was radically and fundamentally opposed by the second most important prophetic writer in the Old Testament. For Jesus to set himself up against Jeremiah is rather like a modern Christian setting himself up against Paul. And there was more to it even than that: within forty years of Jesus' death Jerusalem was (yet again) overwhelmed by just the kind of disaster that Jeremiah here threatens it with. It was already very obvious in Jesus' day that things were moving towards that kind of catastrophe: the people known as Zealots (see Luke 6:15, Acts 1:13 – but also it is likely that the 'Galileans' in Luke 13:1-2 were in fact these Zealots) were already advocating immediate rebellion against Rome in the ludicrous expectation that, if only a start were to be made, the heavens would open and divine forces would array themselves on the side of the Jews to ensure a miraculous and immediate victory (see Matthew 26:53). It is very likely that Jesus did in fact foretell the destruction of Jerusalem as the gospels say he did; but if so, he did it not on the basis of a miraculous knowledge of the mind of God, but as the Old Testament prophets themselves had done it: by taking notice, in an entirely unmiraculous way, of the direction in which history appeared to be moving. His opponents, though, could have pointed out on the basis of Jeremiah's prophecy that with people like him around it was only too likely his prophecy would be fulfiled.

It is admittedly speculative, but nevertheless irresistibly intriguing, to try to reconstruct the original events behind the excerpt from Matthew's gospel with which we opened. The question that will not go away is this: Are we to suppose that the Pharisees followed Jesus and his disciples as they wandered through the cornfields, and there and then protested at what they saw?' This seems to me unlikely. And then again, how many of these disciples were there? The Sunday school answer would be 'Twelve', but when we look at all the material available, that begins to look like an underestimate. The gospels and Acts make it clear that there were twelve 'apostles', but a very much larger, more amorphous body of 'disciples'. In

Luke 10:1 we find there are seventy (or more probably seventy two). In Acts 1:15 we learn that immediately after Jesus' death these 'disciples' numbered 'about a hundred and twenty', and it is likely that at the time there had just been a 'shake-out' from this body of disciples as large numbers of them concluded from the fact of Jesus' death that he was not, after all, the redeemer they had been hoping for. At the lowest estimate, therefore, the raiding party on the Galilean cornfields is likely to have been at least forty or fifty, possibly as many as two hundred.

Moreover, they raided the cornfields in order to satisfy hunger. This does not mean they each plucked one or two ears of corn to see how nice they tasted. Jesus and his followers lived as vagabonds, so that in their case being 'hungry' will have meant being absolutely famished. We can begin to appreciate that the above incident implied very serious loss to the farmer involved, and it seems likely to me that the debate outlined is the substance of some kind of formal proceedings against Jesus and his disciples. An angry farmer rides into town one Sunday morning and lodges a complaint with the religious authorities against Jesus and his disciples that they have devastated his harvest. The disciples are summoned to the synagogue to answer the charge, the decision goes against them and in some way or other they are punished. Jesus loudly protests, quoting Hosea 6:6 at the court to show that they have come to the wrong decision ("And if you had known what this means, 'I desire mercy and not sacrifice', you would not have condemned the guiltless.")

If all this appears more critical of Jesus than the tradition allows, and more supportive of his opponents, that is probably to the good. We should bear in mind that the gospels are in no way to be treated as impartial records of history, and it must often have been the case that where the tradition makes Jesus appear unquestionably right and his adversaries unquestionably wrong, the issues would have been by no means so clear cut to the actual onlookers.

Let us examine the nature of the complaint a little more closely. The disciples are not accused of theft, of which they are not in fact guilty. Had they acted as they did on any other day than the sabbath, they would have been absolutely in the clear:

> "When you go into your neighbour's vineyard, you may eat your fill of grapes, as many as you wish, but you shall not put any in your vessel. When you go into your neighbour's standing grain, you may pluck the ears with your hand, but you shall not put a sickle to your neighbour's standing grain." (Deuteronomy 23:24-25)

Their offence is a more technical one. Plucking the ears of grain was technically reaping, rubbing them in one's hands to seperate the kernel from the husk was threshing, and both these activities were prohibited on the sabbath. If one knows anything about human nature, it was the theft and damage that actually rankled, but the court has to nail the disciples on charges that will actually stick.

What of the probable defence? The quotation. from Hosea (which is found only in Matthew – but twice: here, and also in 9:13 where it seems less appropriate) gives us the best clue we are likely to get. Jesus' objection to the sabbath regulations, as we have seen, appears to have been that they caused needless difficulties; if one encountered suffering on the sabbath day, then one must relieve it on the sabbath day (Luke 13:10-16), there was no need and no point in holding back until sundown. The point is a good one, though in this instance perhaps weakened by the fact that Jesus is talking about his own need, which he seems to have relieved at some one else's expense without consulting them. It is likely, as we shall see in chapter 4, that Jesus, being the sort of person he was, had only a vague notion of private property, which he seems to have viewed as at best an encumbrance, at worst as a misappropriation of God's gifts which were intended to benefit all.

If we find that on this occasion we have more sympathy for Jesus'

The Improper Use of Scripture

opponents than the gospel wishes us to have, this does not undermine the principle for which he was contending, of which the quotation from Hosea is such a brilliant summary. It will pay us to go through the opening excerpt in a little more detail to bring this point out, and also to clean up a few incidental distortions which (as in almost any passage of scripture we put under the magnifying glass) we will be able to detect. Let us compare the passage with the version in Mark – which was not only familiar to Matthew but which, as we can tell from comparison of the two gospels as a whole, he actually had before him as he wrote:

> One sabbath he was going through the grainfields; and as they made their way his disciples began to pluck ears of grain. And the Pharisees said to him, "Look, why are they doing what is not lawful on the sabbath?" And he said to them, "Have you never read what David did, when he was in need and was hungry, he and those who were with him: how he entered the house of God, when Abiathar was high priest, and ate the bread of the Presence, which it is not lawful for any but the priests to eat, and also gave it to those who were with him?" And he said to them, "The sabbath was made for man, not man for the sabbath; so the Son of man is lord even of the sabbath."
>
> (Mark 2:23-28)

Usually when we compare a passage in Mark with the same passage in Matthew the Matthew version is shorter, because Matthew had a lot of material to get into his gospel which Mark seems not to have known about. A comparison of the two versions here gives a good illustration of Matthew's procedures. Although Matthew's version as a whole is longer than Mark's, the bit he 'borrowed' - the reference to David and his followers eating the bread of the Presence - is actually shorter; and then Matthew 12:5-7 consists entirely of material not found in Mark:

> "Or have you not read in the law how on the sabbath the priests in the

temple profane the sabbath and are guiltless? I tell you, something greater than the temple is here. And if you had know what this means, 'I desire mercy, and not sacrifice', you would not have condemned the guiltless."

A very interesting discrepancy is noticed when we compare the conclusion of the two excerpts. For some reason Matthew has omitted the first half of Mark's concluding verse: "The sabbath was made for man, not man for the sabbath."

It will be obvious to anyone reading the first three gospels that all three of them are on the one hand garbled and distorted accounts of the events they describe, but on the other that they do nevertheless contain real reminiscences of an actual historic figure. How do we identify (a) the real reminiscences, and (b) the distortions? However much modern scholarship may pile up the arguments, the references and the apparatus, when we come down to it we do in fact have to guess, and I make no apology for the fact that what follows is largely guesswork.

All three gospels appear to have been written for the use of specific congregations. Even the Theophilus to whom Luke's gospel is addressed must in fact have been a member of a church rather than just a solitary enquirer. The particular bias which interested Mark's congregation is less easy to discover than Luke's and Matthew's, since in his case we have nothing earlier to compare him with. Luke's Theophilus is likely to have been a Gentile convert to Christianity, and the interests of such a person are well reflected in Luke's gospel, particularly in the material about Samaritans. In Mark's gospel there are no references to Samaritans at all, in Matthew there is a single hostile reference (10:5); but in Luke we have three – 9:51-56, 10:30-37 (the story of the Good Samaritan) and 17:11-19. Only the first of these is likely to be authentic; the other two, though undoubtedly edifying, look to the practiced eye to be fictional - indeed it is just because they are so very edifying that one suspects their authenticity. The reason for Luke's readers' interest in Samaritans is easy to understand: the historic Jesus had very little contact with Gentiles as such, and this irreducible fact is the reason why the gospels contain so very little about them. The healing of the Syrophoenician woman's daughter (Mark 7:24-30 = Matthew 15:21-28) is the single explicit instance – which Luke does not include in his gospel undoubtedly because of Jesus' initial unflattering response to the woman's request for help: "Let the children (i.e. Jews) first be fed, for it is not right to take the children's bread and throw it to the dogs (i.e. Gentiles)". Samaritans for Luke's congregation were the nearest substitute for Gentiles he could find, a fact which is also reflected in chapter 8 of Acts.

There is a detectable bias in Matthew's gospel in just the opposite direction – which is initially surprising because, given its likely date (certainly after 70, probably nearer 80 AD), it is hard to believe that any Christian congregation any longer consisted primarily of ethnic Jews, which is very much the impression this gospel actually gives. In this gospel, more even than in Mark's, one learns to one's surprise (but nevertheless it is probably the truth) that Jesus on the whole shared the feelings of his fellow Jews about Gentiles. I am inclined to regard all the following as genuine sayings of Jesus: 5:47, 6:7, 6:32, 20:5 – but only Matthew gives us them. The story of the Gerasene/Gadarene/Gergesene swine (Mark 5:1-20 = Matthew 8:28-34, Luke 8:26-39) probably reflects the same outlook. The likeliest reason why Jesus does not allow the healed man to follow him is that he was not a Jew, but since the anti-Gentile bias is not made explicit here, Luke this time does include the story.

I mention all this because I believe it throws light on verses 5 and 6 of the opening excerpt: "Or have you not read in the law how on the sabbath the priests in the temple profane the sabbath and are guiltless? I tell you, something greater than the temple is here." Neither of these occurs elsewhere in any of the gospels, and I do not believe either of them is genuine. The first sounds to my ears like the kind of thing a congregation engaged in bible study might come up with: "And he could also have pointed out. . ." and so forth. (We should bear in mind there is likely to be a considerable amount of this kind of material in all four of our gospels, even though we can only rarely detect it.) The second looks like a fictive echo of what are apparently genuine sayings recorded later in the same chapter (12:41-42). But when we come to the quotation from Hosea, although this also occurs in no other gospel, I suspect it may well be genuine. It is of course exceedingly apt, which in the eyes of a critic would tend to count against it; but it seems to me to be tied to that other phrase which is unique to Matthew, "...you would not have condemned the guiltless." As was made clear in the early part of this chapter, I see in the word 'condemned' here a reference to an original context which the tradition has suppressed, namely an actual trial of the disciples on a charge of infringing the sabbath. But I stress again, this is largely guesswork which the reader is at liberty to accept or reject as he feels more or less convinced.

For the final comment we turn again to Mark's original account: "The sabbath was made for man, not man for the sabbath; so the Son of man is lord even of the sabbath." Matthew has dispensed with the first half of this saying, but kept the second. Why? The question is more than usually interesting because to the modern eye it is the first part of the saying which is genuine and the second which is more likely to be a claim made on behalf of Jesus by his followers after his death. The reason for the addition appears to be to tone down what the genuine saying implies, which suggests that even Mark's congregation may have been uncomfortable with it; Matthew seems to have found it altogether too anarchic to be acceptable. But it is precisely its anarchic implications which make it likely that it is genuine. The original saying implies that anyone can, and anyone should, dispense with rules that are unnecessary and burdensome; but the addition is meant to suggest that Jesus can do so because of who he is, which seems deliberately intended to cast doubt on whether anyone else may do so. If the sabbath is made for man and not man for the sabbath, can not the same be said for the Scriptures as a whole, indeed for religion as a whole? Indeed it can, and that is why the qualifier is needed - to curb the antinomian implications of the original saying.

What has all this got to do with homosexuality? To most readers I hope it will be obvious. Both the sayings that I have identified as genuine appear to support my case - and yes, it could well be that I have identified them as genuine just because they appear to do so. The Lambeth Conference, like the Pharisees of old, have insisted that God requires sacrifice and not mercy; that the rules are more important than any hardships they impose, that no legitimate question can be raised as to whether they are necessary: if they are *biblical*, the question of whether they are necessary does not arise. But if they had known what this means, "I desire mercy and not sacrifice", so I argue, they would not have condemned the guiltless.

Homosexuality in the Old Testament

WE have heard a great deal about how Scripture 'unambiguously condemns homosexuality throughout both Old and New Testaments'. As regards the Old Testament here is the whole of this 'unambiguous' condemnation:

> You shall not lie with a male as with a woman; It is an abomination.
> (Leviticus 18:22)
> If a man lies with a male as with a woman, both of them have committed an abomination; they shall be put to death, their blood is upon them.
> (Leviticus 20:13)

Chapter 18 of Leviticus (which is somewhat easier for the modern reader to take than the more extreme and punitive chapter 20) is neatly set out and can be conveniently summarized. Verses 1-5 is a preamble which states that in much of what follows Israel's practice is to be more restricted, both in matters of incest (vv.6-18) and of sexual propriety generally (vv.19-23) than is that of those other 'pagan' nations with which Israel comes into frequent contact. The big difference between this and chapter 20 is that in chapter 18 no specific punishment is attached to any of the offences; the chapter concludes (vv.24-30) with a general threat of the disintegration and decline of society as a whole if these practices are tolerated, as many of them are both by the Egyptians and the Canaanites.

If you examine chapter 20 closely, you will find that the actual material is much the same as that of chapter 18, only it is much less clearly arranged, and this time a particular punishment is attached to each particular offence. People offering their children in sacrifice are to be stoned (v.2), and cases of sexual impropriety (rather than incest as such) are to be punished with death – though the manner of death is not specified except in the case of a man marrying a woman and her daughter, in which case all three of them are to be burned alive (v.24): it is possible that in all the cases mentioned in this section (vv.10-16) the intended punishment was burning - see Genesis 38:24, Leviticus 21:9). In the incest section of the chapter (vv.17-21) there are once again punishments attached, but it is by no means clear, except in the last two instances (vv.20, 21) what the punishment is to be. It is not clear, for instance, whether phrases like "they shall be cut off in the sight of the children of their people" (v.17) or "they shall bear their iniquity" (vv.17, 19) mean that they are to be executed or simply left to divine vengeance. If we look back to earlier in the chapter:

> And if the people of the land do at all hide their eyes from that man, when he gives one of his children to Molech, and do not put him to death, then I will set my face against that man and against his family, and will cut them off from among their people. . . .
>
> (Leviticus 20:4-5a)

it is clear that the original meaning, at any rate, referred to God's punishment. One suspects, though, when the phrase is used as often as it is here, that in time God's notorious remissness in carrying out threats of this kind was often made up for by the zeal and anger of man.

The above two short passages, as I say, are the whole of the 'unambiguous' condemnation of homosexuality in the Bible - though I think one must concede that the reticence of Scripture as a whole on the subject is much more because the various authors considered the subject to be unmentionable rather than because they thought it unimportant. What needs to be stressed for the modern reader, however, is the primitiveness and savagery of the Levitical code as a whole. Fundamentalist parsons may be eager to draw attention to the two verses at the head of this chapter as 'proving' that God condemns homosexuality; they would be less eager, I suspect, to read out chapters 18 and 20 in their entirety, which would make their outright condemnation appear (as indeed it is) primitive, pre-civilized, pre-rational.

I have said that the above two verses from Leviticus 18 and 20 are the whole of the unambiguous condemnation of homosexuality in the Old Testament, and strictly speaking this is true. But mention must also be made, obviously, of the story of the destruction of Sodom in Genesis 19:

> The two angels came to Sodom in the evening; and Lot was sitting in the gate of Sodom. When Lot saw them, he rose to meet them, and bowed himself with his face to the earth, and said, "My lords, turn aside, I pray you, to your servant's house and spend the night, and wash your feet; then you may rise up early and go on your way." They said, "No; we will spend the night in the street." But he urged them strongly; so they turned aside to him and entered his house; and he made them a feast, and baked unleavened bread, and they ate. But before they lay down, the men of the city, the men of Sodom, both young and old, all the people to the last man, surrounded the house; and they called to Lot, "Where are the men who came to you tonight? Bring them out to us, that we may know them." Lot went out of the door to the men, shut the door after him, and said, "I beg you, my brothers, do not act so wickedly. Behold, I have two daughters who have not known man; let me bring them out to you, and do to them as you please; only do nothing to these men, for they have come under the shelter of my roof." But they said, "Stand back!" And they said, "This fellow came to sojourn, and he would play the judge! Now we will deal worse with you than with them." Then they pressed hard against the man Lot, and drew near to break the door. But the men put forth their hands and brought Lot into the house to them, and shut the door. And they struck with blindness the men who were at the door of the house, both small and great, so that they wearied themselves groping for the door. (Genesis 19:1-11)

There can be no doubt of the sexual implications of the demand, "Bring them out to us, that we may know them", since there would otherwise be no point in Lot offering his virgin daughters to the mob in their place. But is it really 'sodomy' which is intended as the shocking feature of the story? The question arises because of the very similar incident we find recounted in Judges:

> When they were near Jebus *[i.e. Jerusalem, still a Canaanite city at this time, before its capture by King David]*, the day was far spent, and the servant said to his master, "Come now, let us turn aside to this city of the Jebusites, and spend the night in it." And his master said to him, "We will not turn aside into the city of foreigners who do not belong to the people of Israel; but we will pass on to Gibeah . . . ." And he went in and sat down in the open square of the city; for no man took them into his house to spend the night.
>
> And behold, an old man was coming from his work in the field at evening. . . . And he lifted up his eyes, and saw the wayfarer in the open square of the city; and the old man said, "Where are you going, and whence do you come?" And he said to him, "We are passing from Bethlehem in Judah to the remote parts of the hill country of Ephraim, from which I come. I went to Bethlehem in Judah; and I am going to my home; and nobody takes me into his house. We have straw and provender for our asses, with bread and wine for me and your maidservant *[i.e. his concubine, who will be the victim of the story]* and the young man *[i.e. the servant]* with your servants; there is no lack of anything." And the old man said, "Peace be to you; I will care for all your wants; only do not spend the night in the square." So he brought them into his house, and gave the asses provender; and they washed their feet, and ate and drank.
>
> As they were making their hearts merry, behold, the men of the city, base fellows, beset the house round about, beating on the door; and they said to the old man, the master of the house, "Bring out the man who came into your house, that we may know him. " And the man, the

master of the house, went out to them and said to them, "No, my brethren, do not act so wickedly; seeing that this man has come into my house, do not do this vile thing. Behold, here are my virgin daughter and his *[i.e. the stranger's]* concubine; let me bring them out now. Ravish them and do with them what seems good to you; but against this man do not do so vile a thing." But the men would not listen to him. So the man *[i.e. the stranger]* seized his concubine, and put her out to them; and they knew her and abused her all night until morning. And as the dawn began to break they let her go.

(Judges 19:11-12, 14b-16a, 17-25)

It seems clear that these are two variant versions of a single traditional story. An element of 'sodomy' is common to both, but is this the real point of what we are told? It is much more likely that what is meant to shock us is the violation of the rules of hospitality, more shocking in the second version than in the first because the stranger and his retinue very nearly had to pass the night in the street. The point is worth making because it makes it clear that, although the inhabitants of Sodom could indeed be charged with 'sodomy', this was not the principle reason why their city was destroyed:

Then the LORD rained on Sodom and Gomorrah brimstone and fire from the LORD out of heaven; and he overthrew those cities, and all the valley, and all the inhabitants of the cities, and what grew on the ground . . . And Abraham went early in the morning to the place where he had stood before the LORD (*see* Genesis 18:22-33); and he looked down toward Sodom and Gomorrah and toward all the land of the valley, and behold, and lo, the smoke of the land went up like the smoke of a furnace.

(Genesis 19:24-28)

That's what happens to cities that don't look after their visitors properly! Abusing them, or even the intention of abusing them, is undoubtedly worse than simply neglecting them, but that seems to be an aggravation, rather than the substance, of the offence for which they are punished.

We have now examined all the material in the the Old Testament that relates to homosexuality. Pick up a Bible, hold the pages between your fingers that include Genesis to Malachi (or to II Maccabees if you happen to be a Catholic) and it will astonish you how very little this is in comparison with the whole.

If you happen to be a reader of the Authorized Version (or the Douai version) of the Bible, you will perhaps not be wholly convinced when I claim to have covered all the relevant material dealing with homosexuality. For instance, what about the 'sodomites' mentioned in Deuteronomy 23:17, I Kings 14:24, 15:12, 22:46, II Kings 23:7? Sadly, however, the term is a mistranslation – a very early one which goes back to the Septuagint, the pre-Christian translation of the Hebrew Scriptures into Greek (and which contains more material than the traditional Hebrew Bible, which is why Catholic Bibles to this day contain more material than Protestant ones), but a mistranslation nevertheless. The Hebrew word is *qadesh*, which literally means 'a holy man'; these *q'deshim* were indeed prostitutes, but the interesting point is that their clients appear to have been women, and particularly childless women, who went to them not primarily for sexual pleasure but in the hope of becoming pregnant when they had failed with their husbands. Look for instance, at the following:

> Now Eli the priest was sitting on the seat beside the doorpost of the temple of the LORD. She *[i.e. Hannah, the mother of Samuel]* was deeply distressed and prayed to the LORD, and wept bitterly. And she vowed a vow and said, "O LORD of hosts, if thou wilt indeed look on the affliction of thy maidservant, and remember me, and not forget thy maidservant, but wilt give to thy maidservant a son, then I will give

him to the LORD all the days of his life, and no razor shall touch his head."

As she continued praying before the LORD, Eli observed her mouth. Hannah was speaking in her heart; only her lips moved, and her voice was not heard; therefore Eli took her to be a drunken woman. And Eli said to her, "How long will you be drunken? Put away your wine from you." But Hannah answered, "No, my lord, I am a woman sorely troubled; I have drunk neither wine nor strong drink, but I have been pouring out my soul before the LORD. Do not regard your maidservant as a base woman, for all along I have been speaking out of my great anxiety and vexation." Then Eli answered, "Go in peace, and the God of Israel grant your petition which you have made to him." And she said, "Let your maidservant find favour in your eyes." Then the woman went her way and ate, and her countenance was no longer sad.

(I Samuel 1:9b-18)

It is pretty clear that something has fallen out of the text - or more likely has been deliberately excised - after, "And she said, 'Let your maidservant find favour in your eyes' ", and the likelihood is that she is asking Eli to perform for her, and he did so, and that is why "her countenance was no longer sad". And this seems to have been the function that the *q'deshim* mentioned in the series of texts above were meant to fulfil.

Finally we need to look at the unaccountable relationship that appears to have existed between David and Jonathan. It must be said at once that there is nothing explicitly sexual in the material that has come down to us, though on the other hand we can be sure that if there had been, as in the story of Eli above, it would have long since been edited out. The strangest passage to modern ears is this:

Then Saul's anger was kindled against Jonathan, and he said to him, "You son of a perverse, rebellious woman, do I not know that you have chosen the son of Jesse to your own shame, and to the shame of your mother's nakedness?" (I Samuel 20:30)

It will disappoint some readers, I know, but what he is in fact accusing Jonathan of is political naivety rather than sexual perversity. He is telling him: "You were born to succeed me, yet here you are befriending a man who very obviously has an ambition to become king in your place, if not indeed in mine."

It is entirely obvious from the surviving material that Saul fell out with David as he came to realize the extent of David's ambition; and, bearing in mind that the records we have were created by King David's chroniclers rather than by King Saul's, it is clear also that Saul was justified in his suspicions. But it also seems clear that Jonathan continued his friendship with David long after his father's hostility became known. Why? After all, it is scarcely imaginable that Jonathan was unaware of the reasons for his father's hatred. That is the peculiar circumstance which makes it attractive to suppose that, on Jonathan's part at any rate, there was something passionate about the friendship; but it must be stressed, that is the only specific feature of the story which points in that direction. Even the to our minds perfervid opening of the relationship:

> When he *[i.e. David]* had finished speaking to Saul, the soul of Jonathan was knit to the soul of David, and Jonathan loved him as his own soul . . . Then Jonathan made a covenant with David, because he loved him as his own soul. And Jonathan stripped himself of the robe that was upon him, and gave it to David, and his armour, and even his sword and his bow and his girdle. (I Samuel 18:1, 3-4)

is less significant than some of us might like to think. Up to that point in the story David has been portrayed as a penniless youngest son, and what Jonathan gives him are items which it is to be presumed he could not have provided for himself.

On the other hand, one may sensibly doubt whether David was ever as utterly resourceless as the obviously romantic story of the slaying of Goliath implies he was. In a little regarded passage of the Old Testament (II Samuel 21:19) the slaying of Goliath is attributed to an otherwise unknown Elhanan the son of Jaareoregim - also a Bethlehemite. When we compare David's subsequent fame with Elhanan's subsequent obscurity, we seem bound to accept the deed as more properly credited to Elhanan. In reality David seems to have come to public notice as a spectacularly successful general in Saul's army:

> And David went out and was successful wherever Saul sent him; so that Saul set him aver the men of war. And this was good in the sight of all the people and also in the sight of Saul's servants. (I Samuel 18:5)

and it was no doubt on the basis of the reputation he thus acquired that he conceived the notion of himself becoming king.

How could he have hoped for this? And what was Jonathan's attitude to the gossip that he must have heard going on around him? The surviving records (but remember that they come to us from the hands of King David's scribes) suggest that he approved his friend's ambition:

> And Jonathan, Saul's son, rose and went to David at Haresh, and strengthened his hand in God. And he said to him, "Fear not; for the hand of Saul my father shall not find you; you shall be king over Israel, and I shall be next to you; Saul my father knows this."
> (I Samuel 23:16-17)

It is hard to know whether one ought to believe this. It is just possible that there was a general agreement in Saul's time that whoever was to be king must above all be a successful military leader, and that it was David rather than Jonathan that had this gift. But if that was the case, wouldn't we expect the heir-apparent to feel jealous of his rival rather than regard him with affection?

I have played down, rather than played up, the likelihood of a passionate relationship between the two. The relationship was undoubtedly an emotional one, but on the basis of the material we have we cannot say more than that. On the other hand one must repeat that if it had been more, the surviving records would not have shown it; and it has always been acknowledged by all students of the Old Testament that this relationship was unique in its intensity. The words with which David laments the death of Jonathan are (one must say it) a shocking witness to this intensity:

> I am distressed for you, my brother Jonathan;
>   very pleasant have you been to me.
> Your love to me was wonderful,
>   passing the love of women.
> (II Samuel 1:26)

Homosexuality in the New Testament

ONCE again, the amount of material that concerns us - even in the fabled epistles of Paul - is extremely small; there are at most four references to homosexuality in the New Testament. Let us take the simplest (but also the least certain) first:

> Outside are the dogs and sorcerers and fornicators and murderers and idolators, and every one who loves and practices falsehood.
> (Apocalypse 22:15)

It is extremely likely, though not absolutely certain, that 'dogs' here derives from Deuteronomy 23:17-18. I referred to verse 17 in the previous chapter; here it is again, with the following verse:

> "There shall be no cult prostitute of the daughters of Israel, neither shall there be a cult prostitute of the sons of Israel, You shall not bring the hire of a harlot, or the wages of a dog, into the house of the LORD your God in payment for any vow; for both of these are an abomination to the LORD your God," (Deuteronomy 23:17-18)

Just as the Hebrew for a male 'cult prostitute' is *qadesh*, or 'holy man', so the female version here is *q'deshah* or 'holy woman'. What her function was we can only guess because of the extreme rarity of the word's occurrence; the normal Hebrew word for a 'harlot' is *zonah*, as in the second sentence above. The notable mention of *q'deshah* apart from this passage is in Genesis 38, where Tamar offers herself to Judah, not as a *zonah*, but as a *q'deshah*. To this we should probably conjoin Ruth's act in Ruth 3, a connection that the book itself makes in 4:12. What both these acts have in common is that they took place in the context of some kind of harvest festival, and our best guess (but it is only a guess) is that the *q'deshah* attached herself to the local sanctuary to add to the pleasure of the 'worshippers' at such festivals; in that case her function was more purely one of indulgence than was that of the *qadesh*.

The point to be made (that by 'dogs' the author of the Apocalypse probably meant 'sodomites') will be clearer if I repeat the above excerpt with the relevant Hebrew words substituted where appropriate:

> "There shall be no *q'deshah* of the daughters of Israel, neither shall there be a *qadesh* of the sons of Israel. You shall not bring the hire of a *zonah*, or the wages of a *keleb*, into the house . . ." etc.

where the parallel is clear between the female *q'deshah* or *zonah*, on the one hand, and the male *qadesh* or *keleb* on the other. The author of the Apocalypse will have read his Bible (or, as we call it, the Old Testament) in the Greek translation of the Septuagint where, as we have seen, *qadesh* is translated as *sodomita*; so it is a reasonable inference that 'dogs' in Apocalypse 22:15 is intended to mean 'sodomites', the actual word at the time being considered all but unrepeatable. The same is probably true of Philippians 3:2 where Paul also warns his readers to "look out for the dogs"

The two remaining instances of Paul condemning homosexuality are much more interesting and (most readers will feel) much more to the point. The first, I'm afraid, is rather long:

> For the wrath of God is revealed from heaven against all ungodliness and wickedness of men, who by their wickedness suppress the truth. For what can be known about God is plain to them, because God has shown it to them. Ever since the creation of the world, his invisible nature, namely his eternal power and deity, has been clearly perceived in the things that have been made, So they are without excuse; for although they knew God, they did not honour him as God or give

thanks to him, but they became futile in their thinking and their senseless minds were darkened. Claiming to be wise, they became fools, and exchanged the glory of the immortal God for images resembling mortal man or birds or animals or reptiles.

Therefore God gave them up in the lusts of their hearts to impurity, to the dishonouring of their bodies among themselves, because they exchanged the truth about God for a lie and worshiped and served the creature rather than the Creator, who is blessed for ever! Amen.

For this reason God gave them up to dishonourable passions. Their women exchanged natural relations for unnatural, and the men likewise gave up natural relations with women and were consumed with passion for one another, men committing shameless acts with men and receiving in their own persons the due penalty for their error.

And since they did not see fit to acknowledge God, God gave them up to a base mind and to improper conduct. They were filled with all manner of wickedness, evil, covetousness, malice. Full of envy, murder, strife, deceit, malignity, they are gossips, slanderers, haters of God, insolent, haughty, boastful, inventors of evil, disobedient to parents, foolish, faithless, heartless, ruthless. Though they know God's decree that those who do such things deserve to die, they not only do them but approve those who practice them.   (Romans 1:18-32)

If some of this seems unfair, let us acknowledge also that it is a magnificent piece of invective, and that it is of the nature of invective, considered as a rhetorical art, to be unfair. The unfairness is mostly in the first paragraph; once past that, one can make a very good case for the rest. The argument in brief is that idolatry lies at the root of almost every other wickedness, and the kind of idolatry Paul is thinking of is indicated in the close of the first paragraph; and this presents us with a problem. One assumes, and everything in the second and third paragraphs points in that direction, that it was Greek idolatry he had in mind; but the Greeks never imagined their gods as "birds or animals or reptiles". The Egyptians did, and debased forms of Egyptian religion were widely familiar throughout the Levant, where Paul chiefly operated. Is he being just careless, or actually malicious, in lumping the two together without distinction? Probably (it must be said) malicious, because he also lumps two sorts of Greek paganism together, clearly with malicious intent. In the Greek world there were basically two forms of religion, that of the philosophers and that of the populace. The philosophers (wiser than those of the modern West) outwardly conformed to popular religion, but understood it and interpreted it in a very different way. The people at large believed the mythology of Greek religion to be 'true', without much going into the question (one suspects, rather like modern Fundamentalist religion) of what it means to claim that something is true. The philosophers on the whole were tacitly agreed that there wasn't a word of truth in any of it. Some would nevertheless regard it as benign, and claim that the stories were useful images of abstract ideas which could be upheld as true; but there were plenty of others who would unhesitatingly have agreed with Paul that much of the imagery was gross and carnal, and that it also encouraged grossness and carnality in the people who were brought up on it. That's where the real unfairness of the first paragraph lies; Paul makes no distinction between philosophical and popular paganism, and even suggests ("Claiming to be wise, they became fools, and exchanged the glory of the immortal God for images...") that popular paganism is a consequence of philosophical paganism, which is wickedly untrue.

Before we go on to examine the remaining argument, I would like to add a couple of footnotes. The Romans, who presided over all this, by and large took the philosophers' view that there wasn't a word of truth in any of it. But they also regarded religion (in my view quite rightly) as an essential mechanism for stabilizing society. Their solution was to allow philosophers absolute freedom, both in their writings and in their talk *among themselves,* to say what they liked. The barrier of literacy was strong enough in those days to ensure that very little of the disturbing opinions of philosophers ever reached a wider audience. Christians got it in the neck from the Roman authorities because of their alarming success in breaking down that barrier; their aim was to convince everybody that there was no truth in popular paganism, and they put their ideas into writings that were fairly accessible even to the unintelligent. The fact that in Roman eyes what Christians claimed to be true was no truer, was indeed much more grossly superstitious, than what they condemned as false, was not the major consideration; what they objected to was *any* disturbance of popular belief. The other point concerns the religion of Egypt. When Paul condemns images of God "resembling...birds or animals or reptiles", it is hard to avoid the supposition that Egyptian mythology is what he is referring to. Yet the big criticism he is going to make of idolatry is the sexual licence it encourages. Why then does he make no mention of a common Egyptian practice of his day which we still find horrifying – the widespread acceptance of brother/sister marriages?

But to return to the text. "Therefore God gave them up in the lusts of their hearts to impurity, to the dishonouring of their bodies among themselves…" This will strike modern readers as an unfair inference but, as we have seen above, there would have been many of Paul's pagan contemporaries who agreed with him that the licentiousness of Greek mythology encouraged the licentiousness of the worshippers. The phrase "to the dishonouring of their bodies among themselves" translates fairly well into the modern notion of "recreational sex", and this of course raises the question for us (though it is unlikely to have done so for most of Paul's contemporaries) whether such "recreational sex" is not in fact a thoroughly good thing. If 'liberation' is your watchword, then it probably seems that it is; otherwise I suspect not. The question is better discussed in the following chapter; for the moment we observe that a good case can be made for Paul's linking of Greek mythology with sexual abandonment.

It is this sexual abandonment which enables the appearance of what Paul no doubt considered to be sexual perversity, the practice of lesbianism between women (verse 26) and of homosexuality between men (verse 29

– though what he meant by the words, "…and receiving in their own persons the due penalty for their error" is very hard to see. He seems to mean that they suffered some nasty physical consequences; perhaps, being a virgin himself, he was naive enough to suppose that venereal diseases only affected homosexuals, as in our day there are still those who think that AIDS is exclusively a homosexual disease). Once again, if we set aside the loaded term 'sexual perversity', the observation is probably just. References to lesbianism are hard to find in Greek mythology; just possibly Diana's attitude to her virgin attendants can be taken as an instance of *mental* lesbianism, but all the stories make it pretty clear that for her no men means no sex of any kind. It was the poetry of Sappho (born about 612 BC) that seems to have provided the bannerhead for the liberated lesbian women in the ancient world. Stories of the (male) homosexual loves of the gods, on the other hand, are almost too numerous to mention: Zeus and Ganymede, Apollo and Hyacinth, Hercules and Hylas, as well as the heroes Achilles and Patroclus, provided all the justification any man needed for proclaiming his sexual preference for boys over girls. The greater prestige of the male models for homosexuality over the female no doubt reflects the more restricted lives of women in antiquity compared with that of men.

The final paragraph of the excerpt is the one that modern readers will find hardest to take, despite the fact that our world, more than any in humanity's previous history (including that of Paul's own time) provides the strongest justification for Paul's argument. What he seems to have in mind is that the lack of restraint in sexual matters leads to a lack of restraint generally, since the bonds of society are essentially an enlargement of the bonds of the family. He seems to be arguing that the kind of sexual freedom going on around him has a tendency to dissolve the ties of loyalty and fidelity that are the very basis of marriage and the family, and this in turn dissolves the bonds of society as a whole. However much we may enjoy modern freedoms, it is all but impossible to deny that they have inflicted enormous damage on the institution of marriage, and this in turn has created whole armies of youngsters growing up without supervision, without ties of loyalty and affection except those they have chosen for themselves (often of a dubious nature), and without any element of moral education in their upbringing. There will be plenty of media persons to insist that there is really nothing new in all this, that there have always been 'disfunctional' families, and therefore disaffected, antisocial, and frequently violent and criminal, young men. Yes, that has always been the case; what is new is the scale on which we allow this to happen and the complacency with which we accept the situation, in contrast to the alarm which previous generations have always felt and acted upon.

Have I come to bury Paul or to praise him? Aren't I supposed to be criticizing his views on homosexuality? Yes, indeed, but it is a good plan when criticizing an opponent, to state his case fairly at the outset (although I also concede that throughout history the Christian church has never been fond of this procedure). I have said all that is to be said on behalf of Paul's views; what now is to be said against them?

The first point to note is that Paul seems to write almost on the assumption (as has the Christian church until very recent times) that we can *choose* whether to be homosexual or not. He seems to suggest that homosexuality arises from unbounded licence rather than anyone's innate condition. On the other hand, he is well aware that there are many for whom total abstinence from sex is simply not a possibility:

> To the unmarried and the widows I say that it is well for them to remain single as I do. But if they cannot exercise self-control, they should marry. For it is better to marry than to be aflame with passion.
>
> (I Corinthians 7:8-9)

Or again:

> If anyone thinks that he is not behaving properly toward his betrothed, if his passions are strong and it has to be, let him do as he wishes: let them marry – it is no sin. (I Corinthians 7:36)

Is it only heterosexuals who are under this kind of compulsion? Why should we think so? And if not, why is the same remedy not available to homosexuals as to others? In what way is marriage undermined by making provision for homosexuals also to find partners and to live quiet, domestic, decorous, sex lives? It may be argued that most homosexuals don't want any such thing; they actually want the excitement and restlessness of the sordid promiscuity they generally pursue. Supposing this is true, is that a reason for making difficulties for the minority who don't? When I was young, it was impossible for a homosexual to admit to his condition at all in any but one circumstance. No, not privacy – one couldn't generally trust even one's closest friends with such a dreadful secret; the only circumstance in which one could admit to being homosexual was in situations of a scarcely imaginable depravity. Such was the situation that Christian condemnation over the centuries had brought about, and such is the situation that would recurr if Fundamentalist condemnation were to become widespread once again.

I do not give much credence to the idea that there is a detectable gene which causes homosexuality; that sounds to me like a laboratory freak looking for a reputation. But one thing is certain: one does not choose to become a homosexual; one discovers that one is. Even the church seems ready to admit this nowadays, and such an admission removes the whole basis for the traditional condemnation. It is not God that requires homosexuals, unlike other men, to lead lives of chastity, but a parson, or a collection of parsons. And what hope do parsons have that anyone is even going to try to live without sex, and for no other reason than that a parson told them to?

The second passage of Paul's writings that we must look at in detail is this:

> Do you not know that the unrighteous will not inherit the kingdom of God? Do not be deceived; neither the immoral, nor idolaters, nor

adulterers, nor homosexuals, nor thieves, nor the greedy, nor revilers, nor robbers will inherit the kingdom of God. (I Corinthians 6:9-10)

I will be chiefly interested in examining what he means by the phrase "inherit the kingdom of God", but before I go on to do that I need to raise questions about the word 'homosexuals' here. A marginal note in the RSV tells us that, "Two Greek words are rendered by this expression", and the two words in question are *malakoi* and *arsenokoitai*. The *malakoi* ('softies') are passive homosexuals, and the *arsenokoitai* ('those who lie with men') active. Paul mentions both specifically because, in the culture of his day, the role of passive homosexual was considered - no, not immoral so much as rather ridiculous; one lost dignity and standing by being known to be pathic. Former slaves, no matter how wealthy and influential they might later become, could never entirely lose the 'stain' of having gratified their masters in this way; it was entirely taken for granted they had done so. What seems terribly unjust to us is that the slave, who gratified his master under the threat of unimaginable penalties for even thinking of resisting, incurred opprobrium, whereas the master incurred none. So long as one was the active partner in a sex encounter, it scarcely mattered what was the sex, age or condition of the other, one suffered no loss of honour or esteem; on the other hand, the only person who could submit to a man's embrace without any sort of disgrace was his legal wife. In the case of homosexuality Paul rejects this distinction - both partners are equally 'guilty' - and I dare say many of us would praise him for it.

But then, what about this phrase "inherit the kingdom of God"? What dreadful penalty is here being denounced against "immoral . . . idolators . . . adulterers . . . homosexuals" and so forth? Does Paul really mean that when such people die they will not go to heaven? In fact we have a pretty good idea of what he means, and it doesn't seem to be anything like that at all. Perhaps the most authentic of all the sayings attributed to Jesus in the gospels is this:

> "Truly, I say to you, there are some standing here who will not taste death before they see the kingdom of God come with power."
>
> (Mark 9: 1)

What Jesus is prophesying here (and it seems certain that he really did so) is that he will return to earth to set up his kingdom while many of his present hearers are still alive. The original prophecy may have been even more mind-boggling than that; there is a passage in I Corinthians which makes it clear that at one time Paul assumed that everyone would still be alive at Jesus' return to earth:

> Let a man examine himself, and so eat of the bread and drink of the cup. For anyone who eats and drinks without discerning the body eats and drinks judgment upon himself. That is why many of you are weak and ill, and some have died. (I Corinthians 11:28-30)

The inference here is that those that have died have actually missed out on the kingdom of God, which will be inherited only by those still alive at the time of its inauguration. Bearing mind that even Mark's gospel (the earliest) was probably written some time after Paul's death, it may well be that this was in fact Jesus' original prophecy, which has been subsequently modified as well-liked members of the Christian church began to die off. At no point in his writings does Paul ever abandon his belief that he himself will be alive at the time of Christ's appearance. This appears to be the latest view he ever committed to paper:

> Lo! I tell you a mystery. We shall not all sleep, but we shall all be changed, in a moment, in the twinkling of an eye, at the last trumpet. For the trumpet will sound, and the dead will be raised imperishable, and we shall be changed. (I Corinthians 15:51-52)

In other words, those that have died will after all inherit the kingdom, but many of the rest of us will still be alive. (We should not assume, by the way, that this excerpt and the previous one, though they now occur in the single document we know as I Corinthians, originally had any connection with each other. It is very evident to anyone reading the epistles to the Corinthians straight through that they are both made up of fragments of letters which were originally many more than two.) The dead will be raised with imperishable bodies, and we that are still alive will suddenly find ourselves miraculously changed from mortal to immortal bodies. When Paul says he is telling us a mystery, he does not mean that what he is saying is in any way hard to understand; he means that the 'information' came to him by direct revelation. The whole of the above, and what follows to the end of the chapter, is in fact perfectly intelligible once we abandon the wholly unnecessary obligation to find a meaning that we can actually believe to be true. History has shown Paul's belief to be groundless; it has not in any way made it hard to understand.

So then it is true that homosexuals will not inherit the kingdom of God, but let them take comfort from the fact that neither will nor has anybody else. Paul died without inheriting it in the way he meant, so have all the saints as well as all the sinners. One should not hurry to be scornful, though. No society can afford totally to abandon the idea of there being a reward for virtue; and on the other hand, no society has ever succeeded in stating convincingly what it is. The Old Testament tries time and again to reward the virtuous, sometimes with riches and honour (I Kings 3:13), sometimes with long life (Exodus 20:12). The Psalmist had never seen "the righteous forsaken, or his children begging bread", but commentators seem generally to agree that he must have gone round with his eyes closed. Occasionally we do hear the shocking truth:

> "For you say, 'Where is the house of the prince?
>   Where is the tent in which the wicked dwelt?'

> Have you not asked those who travel the roads,
>> and do you not accept their testimony,
> that the wicked man is spared in the day of calamity,
>> that he is rescued in the day of wrath?
> Who declares his way to his face,
>> and who requites him for what he has done?
> When he is borne to the grave,
>> watch is kept over his tomb.
> The clods of the valley are sweet;
>> all men follow after him,
>> and those who go before him are are innumerable.
>
> (Job 21:28-33)

or:

> There is a vanity which takes place on earth, that there are righteous men to whom it happens according to the deeds of the wicked, and there are wicked men to whom it happens according to the deeds of the righteous.   (Ecclesiastes 8:14)

Such words are no doubt thrilling to the artist, but they are entirely useless to the moralist; nor should we understand the role of the moralist as being either intentionally deceitful (though throughout history no doubt many moralists have been) nor practically useless (and again, the same applies). When Ecclesiastes cries out, "Vanity of vanities! All is vanity!", he means that accurate observation of the human condition shows it to have no meaning or purpose; and, it must be said again, he is right about that, but quite uselessly so. For if our situation does not provide us with a meaning and a purpose, we have to create one for ourselves both as individuals and as a society. Any moral sense at all derives from a view of what we ourselves are 'meant' to be like, or what society as a whole is 'meant' to be like. If our sense of purpose seems to the outsider to be illusory - even if we can see that for ourselves - this would not be grounds for abandoning it; the choice in that case (and I believe this to be our true situation) is between an illusory sense of purpose and no sense of purpose at all. One must add that whatever meaning or purpose modern secularism tries to find in human existence (though on the whole it seems to fight shy of even considering the question), these notions are just as contrived, just as transparently illusory, as any of the traditional religious notions it congratulates itself on having outgrown.

So then Paul turns out to have been wrong, but anyone who has ever tried to guide us in the path of virtue will in time turn out to have been wrong. It is not he that must be criticized, but those who insist on denying that he ever was or ever could be wrong. (Honesty, though, compels one to concede that he himself took something like that view: see I Corinthians 2:16, 7:25 and 40b, 11:16.) It may be that homosexuality is wrong, but if it is, it must be for other reasons than that of Paul having said it was; it may be that it leads to dreadful consequences, but if so Paul clearly failed to discover what they were. So if Fundamentalists are determined to condemn homosexuality, like the Pharisees who condemned the disciples, they must find other grounds than simply that of what the Bible says.

Jesus and Liberation *versus* Paul and Constraint

> For freedom Christ has set us free; stand fast therefore, and do not submit again to a yoke of slavery. (Galatians 5:1)

> For you were called to freedom, brethren; only do not use your freedom as an opportunity for the flesh... (Galatians 5:13)

There can be no doubt that Paul believed in all sincerity that he had found freedom in the gospel of Christ; but to anyone reading his writings, and even more to anyone viewing his modern disciples, this freedom has a dubious quality. Even Paul occasionally admits that there's a catch:

> "All things are lawful for me", but not all things are helpful. "All things are lawful for me", but I will not be enslaved by anything *[and he goes on to talk specifically about sex with prostitutes]*. (I Corinthians 6:12)

> Only take care lest this liberty of yours *[for eating meat that had originally been offered in sacrifice in pagan temples]* somehow become a stumbling block to the weak. (I Corinthians 8:9)

> "All things are lawful", but not all things are helpful. "All things are lawful", but not all things build up. *[And again he goes on to talk about eating meat originally offered to idols]*. (I Corinthians 10:23)

So this Christian liberty that Paul has discovered and feels so wonderful about is not quite what his hearers might have originally assumed. One question needs to be asked immediately: in those three excerpts from I Corinthians is Paul addressing himself primarily to Jewish converts, or rather to pagans? I think we must assume the latter. Initially no pagan would have doubted that, either in the matter of sex or that of diet, "All things are lawful for me"; he would have assumed that from birth, and would perhaps be a little put out to find suddenly that although everything was still 'lawful', there were some things that must be considered no longer 'helpful' – i.e. they weren't actually forbidden, but they might just as well be.

To the unconverted pagan, using the services of a prostitute had no moral significance at all; and even less, of course, did eating meat offered in sacrifice to pagan gods. Paul himself is not worried by the second point and agrees there is no reason why anybody should be, but feels constrained by the fact that, regardless of whether they should be or not, some people definitely are. Paul enjoins that out of consideration for such people, one should not knowingly eat such meat in their presence. In no way, on the other hand, is he trying to reimpose the diet restrictions of Leviticus 11 or Deuteronomy 14 on his hearers; if the epistle to the Galatians is anything to go by, Paul probably taught that people who still had a conscience about that should be rebuked for it.

So why this thing, Paul's readers may have wondered, about prostitutes? Taking Paul's writings as a whole, the answer is clear: in the first place, Paul thinks that pagan attitudes to marriage (as we saw in the previous chapter) are far too frivolous, and on the whole the Fundamentalist tradition faithfully represents Paul's view. The big exception is Paul's belief that to be single is preferable to being married:

> Now concerning the unmarried, I have no command of the Lord, but I give my opinion as one who by the Lord's mercy is trustworthy. I think that in view of the impending distress *[i.e, the imminent return of Christ to earth, with the attendant "wars and rumours of wars" – see Mark chapter 13]* it is well for a person to remain as he is. Are you bound to a wife? Do not seek to be free. Are you free from a wife? Do not seek marriage. But if you marry, you do not sin, and if a girl marries she does not sin. Yet those who marry will have worldly troubles, and I

would spare you that. I mean, brethren, the appointed time has grown very short; from now on, let those who have wives live as though they had none, and those who mourn as though they were not mourning, and those who rejoice as though they were not rejoicing, and those who buy as though they had no goods, and those who deal with the world as though they had no dealings with it. For the form of this world is passing away.

I want you to be fee from anxieties. The unmarried man is anxious about the affairs of the Lord, how to please the Lord; but the married man is anxious about worldly affairs, how to please his wife, and his interests are divided. And the unmarried woman or girl is anxious about the affairs of the Lord, how to be holy in body and spirit; but the married woman is anxious about worldly affairs, how to please her husband. I say this for your own benefit, not to lay any restraint upon you, but to promote good order and to secure your undivided devotion to the Lord.

If any one thinks that he is not behaving properly toward his betrothed, if his passions are strong and it has to be, let him do as he wishes: let them marry – it is no sin. But whoever is firmly established in his heart, being under no necessity but having his desire under control, and has determined this in his heart, to keep her as his betrothed, he will do well. So that he who marries his betrothed does well; and he who refrains from marriage will do better.

(I Corinthians 7:25-38)

This is the one point on which the Fundamenalist tradition differs from its teacher. Paul clearly held that celibacy was morally superior to marriage, and the Catholic tradition has always followed him on this point, though not always with happy consequences; Protestants, perhaps the more so because the Catholic tradition praises celibacy, have always stressed the superior virtue of marriage. A grudging role for celibacy has been introduced only in very recent times, where it is allowed that for naturally homosexual men and women celibacy is the preferred and praiseworthy condition. (To paraphrase the above, if their passions are strong and it has to be, let them stay single – it is no sin!) But let me stress that this is a very recent innovation. Only twenty or thirty years ago there was still a total insistance that either there was no such thing as a natural homosexual, or that to be homosexual - whether by nature or by choice - was an unmentionable and unpardonable sin. Some Evangelicals will nowadays *privately* speculate whether Paul praised celibacy because he was himself homosexual (and could that by any chance be the "thorn in the flesh, a messenger of Satan to harass me, to keep me from being too elated" that we read of in II Corinthians 12:7?); but none has yet found the courage to give such disturbing notions public utterance.

Apart from that, it has to be granted that the Protestant tradition faithfully follows Paul's view of marriage and the family: that is to say, sex is permissible only within marriage, which is why not only homosexuality but even sex before marriage, and also going with prostitutes, is totally prohibited for the faithful Christian. Traditionally Protestantism has viewed celibacy with suspicion as being "contrary to nature" and the consequences of that view have on the whole been benign; but, even though much less "contrary to nature" than celibacy, the above still does considerable violence to what most of us think as the natural condition of mankind, and can still be responsible for a very great deal of needless frustration and suffering. And the Fundamentalist tradition is also still at the stage of congratulating itself on being sufficiently enlightened to admit homosexuals to the community on condition of celibacy; it has not yet begun to ask itself why that also should not be considered "contrary to nature", with much the same long-term disadvantages arising from it as from any other form of celibacy.

We know nothing whatever about Jesus' views of sex, since in the surviving records he never mentions the topic. But we know quite a lot about his views of family life, and they are not at all the same as those of Fundamenalist tradition, or indeed of any Christian body throughout history. It is a surprising fact that the overwhelming majority of references to the family throughout the gospels are most naturally interpreted as hostile, and this is even truer of the (admittedly only two) references by Jesus to his mother. It would be going too far to insist that the evidence actually demands this interpretation, but the point must still be made that the natural interpretation is that Jesus had quarrelled with his family, and felt a particular animus towards his mother. If I now simply list the relevant passages below without further comment, for most readers the point will be made:

> "Brother will deliver up brother to death, and the father his child, and children will rise against parents and have them put to death; and you will be hated by all for my name's sake." (Matthew 10:21-22a)

> "For I have came to set a man against his father, and a daughter against her mother, and a daughter-in-law against her mother-in-law; and a man's foes will be those of his own household. He who loves father or mother more than me is not worthy of me; and he who loves son or daughter more than me is not worthy of me . . ."
> (Mathew 10:35-37 – verses 35-36 are a paraphrase of Micah 7:6)

While he was still speaking to the people, behold, his mother and his brothers stood outside, asking to speak to him. But he replied to the man who told him, "Who is my mother, and who are my brothers?" And stretching out his hand towards his disciples, he said, "Here are my mother and my brothers! For whoever does the will of my Father in heaven is my brother, and sister, and mother."
(Matthew 12:46-50 = Mark 3:31-35 = Luke 8:19-21)

Then Peter said in reply, "Lo, we have left everything and followed you. What then shall we have?" Jesus said to them, "Truly, I say to you, in the new world, when the Son of man shall sit on his glorious throne, you

who have followed me will also sit on twelve thrones, judging the twelve tribes of Israel. And every one who has left houses or brothers or sisters or father or mother or children or lands, for my name's sake, will receive a hundredfold, and inherit eternal life.
(Matthew 19:27-29 = Mark 10:28-30 = Luke 18:28-30)

"And call no man your father on earth, for you have one Father, who is in heaven." (Matthew 23:9)

As they were going along the road, a man said to him, "I will follow you whatever you go". And Jesus said to him, "Foxes have holes, and birds of the air have nests; but the Son of man has nowhere to lay his head". To another he said, "Follow me". But he said, "Lord, let me first go and bury my father" [*that is*, "Let me wait until after my father has died"]. But he said to him, "Leave the dead to bury their own dead; but as for you, go and proclaim the kingdom of God". Another said, "I will follow you, Lord; but let me first say farewell to those at my home". Jesus said to him, "No one who puts his hand to the plough and looks back is fit for the kingdom of God".
(Luke 9:57-62 - verses 57-60 = Matthew 8:19-22)

As he said this, a woman in the crowd raised her voice and said to him, "Blessed is the womb that bore you, and the breasts that you sucked!" But he said, "Blessed rather are those who hear the word of God and keep it!" (Luke 11:27-28)

"Do you think that I have come to give peace on earth? No, I tell you, but rather division; for henceforth in one house there will be five divided, three against two and two against three; they will be divided, father against son and son against father, mother against daughter and daughter against her mother, mother-in-law against her daughter-in-law and daughter-in-law against her mother-in-law."
(Luke 12:51-53 = Matthew 10:34-36 above)

> Now great multitudes accompanied him; and he turned and said to them, "If any one comes to me and does not hate his own father and mother and wife and children and brothers and sisters, yes, and even his own life, he cannot be my disciple". (Luke 14:25-26)

Paul has *slight* misgivings about marriage because it necessarily loads the partners with worldly concerns, but he certainly enjoins it rather than condemns it. But Jesus seems to have thought of it as a major obstacle to anyone finding true 'life' at all. (And he does not at all mean, by the way, any form of "life after death"; though he probably does mean "eternal life" in the sense that those who inherit his kingdom will do so while still alive and will never subsequently die). Both of them were aware that not everyone is capable of chastity. Paul's view of that has been quoted above; here is Jesus':

> "And I say to you: whoever divorces his wife, except for unchastity, and marries another, commits adultery."
> The disciples said to him, "If such is the case of a man with his wife, it is not expedient to marry". But he said to them, "Not all men can receive this precept, but only those to whom it is given . . ."
> (Matthew 19:9-11)

(The words "except for unchastity" do not occur in the parallel passage in Mark and are probably not authentic; they have probably been added by 'popular demand' for a later congregation, perhaps specifically for the very one for which 'Matthew' wrote.) Paul, then, is on the whole marriage friendly, and by and large (with the single exception noted above) the Fundamentalist tradition can honestly claim to be following him; but Jesus doesn't seem to have been at all marriage friendly. Jesus and his disciples (as we shall see below) seem to have lived the lives of vagabonds, and Jesus seems to have believed in all seriousness that the life of a vagabond was *morally* superior, and very greatly superior, to that of a married man owning property, earning his living and raising a family. If a man wants to find 'life' he must be ready to jettison all these things.

Neither Paul nor Jesus, as we have seen, had any idea of the need to continue the human race, both of them being utterly convinced that any need for that was now in the past since the world was about to come to an end. Thus even Paul seems to regard marriage more in the light of a "remedy against sin and to avoid fornication" (as the Prayer Book used to have it) than as being "ordained for the procreation of children", which has traditionally been understood as its primary purpose.

The second point on which Paul and Jesus differ (and on which the Fundamentalist tradition *wholly* differs from Jesus) is in the matter of earning one's living. For Paul this is a *moral* obligation:

> Now we command you, brethren, in the name of our Lord Jesus Christ, that you keep away from any brother who is living in idleness and not in accord with the tradition that you received from us. For you yourselves know how you ought to imitate us; we were not idle when we were with you, we did not eat any one's bread without paying, but with toil and labour we worked night and day that we might not burden any of you. It was not because we have not that right, but to give you in our conduct an example to imitate. For even when we were with you, we gave you this command: If any one will not work, let him not eat. For we hear that some of you are living in idleness, mere busybodies, not doing any work. Now such persons we command and exhort in the Lord Jesus Christ to do their work in quietness and to earn their own living. (II Thessalonians 3:6-12)

Like the Fundamentalists themselves I approve of every word of this, but there is no hiding from the fact that Jesus himself would have found it abhorrent. Nothing could be more unfortunate than that exhortation "in the Lord Jesus Christ to do their work...and to earn their own living". We have to remember that Paul died before any of the existing gospels were written, and the likelihood is that he simply didn't know a lot of the material that survives in them. He never refers to any of it in his letters (but then neither do any of the other 'epistles' with the exception of the apparently very late II Peter); he invariably talks about both the crucifixion and the resurrection (the only two incidents of the gospels that seem to have any interest at all for him) as if they were semi-mythical events which are directly experienced in the lives of Christians rather than past events known about through history. Here is what Jesus actually thought about earning one's living:

> "Therefore I tell you, do not be anxious about your life, what you shall eat or what you shall drink, nor about your body, what you shall put on. Is not life more than food, and the body more than clothing? Look at the birds of the air: they neither sow nor reap nor gather into barns, and yet your heavenly Father feeds them. Are you not of more value than they? And which of you by being anxious can add one cubit to his span of life? And why are you anxious about clothing? Consider the lilies of the field, how they grow; they neither toil nor spin; yet I tell you, even Solomon in all his glory was not arrayed like one of these. But if God so clothes the grass of the field, which today is alive and tomorrow is thrown into the oven, will he not much more clothe you, O you of little faith? Therefore do not be anxious, saying, 'What shall we eat?' or 'What shall we drink?' or 'What shall we wear?' For the Gentiles seek all these things; and your heavenly Father knows that you need them all. But seek first his kingdom and his righteousness, and all these things shall be yours as well.
>
> "Therefore do not be anxious about tomorrow, for tomorrow will be anxious for itself. Let the day's own trouble be sufficient for the day."
>
> (Matthew 6:25-34)

The third point on which there is a rift, probably between Jesus and Paul, but certainly between Jesus and the Fundamentalist tradition, is their attitude to low company. This is slightly more difficult to illustrate than the other two because it very much looks as though Jesus' original attitude has already been heavily distorted in the gospel account. The evangelists themselves, or the congregations from whose oral recollections they drew their material, seem to have shared Pharisaic misgivings about Jesus' apparent liking for dissolute parties and to have tidied it up to make it look more 'edifying'. Consider the following:

> And as he sat at table in his house, many tax collectors and sinners were sitting with Jesus and his disciples; for there were many who followed him. And the scribes of the Pharisees, when they saw that he was eating with sinners and tax collectors, said to his disciples, "Why does he eat with tax collectors and sinners?" And when Jesus heard it, he said to them, "Those who are well have no need of a physician, but those who are sick; I came not to call the righteous, but sinners."
> (Mark 2:15-17 = Matthew 9:10-13, Luke 5:29-32)

(Two small points before we go on to the substance of the excerpt. In the English versions of the gospels Jesus and his friends always 'sit' at table, but in the original Greek they in fact recline. The second point is this: In all three gospels the incident immediately follows the calling of Levi (in Mark and Luke) or Matthew (in Matthew). Luke's version stresses that the incident took place in Levi's house, which is not implausible; but then, in Luke's gospel (only) "the Son of man has nowhere to lay his head" (Luke 9:58). Mark on the other hand implies that Jesus in fact owned a house in Capernaum, and that this is where the incident occurred. Matthew hedges his bets by altering Mark's 'his house' (above) to 'the house' (Matthew 9:10).

There is something about this incident that is not quite right in the telling. I can believe that Jesus had a party in his house with disreputable guests, and that this attracted criticism; I can also believe that in some other context his reply quoted here is authentic. What I cannot believe is that this is the authentic context for this saying. This may well be another of those occasions when Jesus fell foul of the local religious authorities – I suspect there were a good many of them – and had to appear before some kind of tribunal to give an answer. Had he in fact been conducting a prayer meeting, no matter how low and disreputable the congregation, it will take more than the gospels to persuade me that the Pharisees would have been anything other than encouraging. Their criticism can only have been on the grounds that it was a rowdy and prolonged celebration which gave considerable annoyance to neighbours. And Jesus' relationship with the disreputable generally seems to have been that of a table companion rather than that of an evangelist, and this is what gave offence to his contemporaries (as indeed it would to any of us today). Jesus at heart was a vagabond and preached the virtues of a carefree, vagabond existence. But long before the gospels came to be written, besides transforming itself from a primarily Jewish into a primarily Gentile sect, the Christian community had become a congregation of householders who by and large shared the Pharisaic point of view; and that is why Jesus' liking for disreputable company has had to be represented as a concern for their spiritual welfare.

Picking and Choosing

THIS will be a short chapter, in that much of the material that properly belongs to it has already been presented in the previous chapter. Some of the points to be made will also strike the reader as being trivial, if not actually frivolous; that is because the claims that are being opposed are often hard to take seriously anyway. The two basic claims of Fundamentalists are first that they believe the whole of the Bible, and not just bits and pieces – and not just the 'nice' bits either; the second is that they believe the Bible to be literally true, and will have nothing to do with the liberal tradition of 'explaining things away'. But while they accuse their opponents of "picking and choosing", it can easily be shown that they themselves are pickers and choosers, and indeed that it is impossible to be otherwise. The book has yet to be written that can truly be regarded in the way Fundamentalists say they regard the Bible; an honest person reading it is forced to admit that not everything in it is good, and also that very little of it can in fact be believed literally. To insist on denying this is stupid, and to insist on denying this when one is not in fact that stupid (as is mostly the case at least with the Fundamentalist clergy) is a serious breach of morality.

I will begin by drawing attention to the implications for the present chapter of what was said in the previous one. "Is Christ divided?", Paul asks in I Corinthians 1:13, and the answer seems to be, "Yes, apparently he is". It is easy to show that whereas Jesus' original disciples were unpropertied vagabonds, Paul appears to have preached his gospel to what we would nowadays call the respectable working classes – where throughout history, and particularly since the rise of Protestantism, it seems to have had its chief appeal. It is this tradition that Fundamentalists tend to follow, in preference to the easy-riding, devil-may-care, take-no-thought-for-the-morrow gospel that Jesus himself originally preached. I would be the last person to criticize them for doing so, but it does mean that they, just like those whom they regard as their opponents, are pickers and choosers of Scripture; by no means do they regard the whole of it as being ' helpful' .

Within that preference it can be conceded they follow Paul on the whole very faithfully, but there is one notable point on which in recent years they have felt obliged to disagree. Paul's views on the role of women in church are well known, and to the modern Fundamentalist increasingly embarassing:

> As in all the churches of the saints *[he simply means specifically Christian, as against unconverted Jewish, congregations]* the women should keep silence in the churches. For they are not permitted to speak, but should be subordinate, as even the law says *[i.e. the traditional religious law of the Jews, though there is no Old Testament passage which ever mentions this subject]*. If there is anything they desire to know, let them ask their husbands at home. For it is shameful for a woman to speak in church. What! Did the word of God originate with you, or are you the only ones it has reached?
>
> (I Corinthians 14:33b-36)

Admittedly Paul does not threaten that women who speak in church "will not inherit the kingdom of God", but he clearly feels very strongly on the subject nevertheless; increasingly in recent years even his most ardent followers among Fundamentalists have quietly agreed to set the passage aside.

If one is going to talk about something that is 'repeatedly condemned' throughout the Old Testament, and whose condemnation is reaffirmed in the New, it would first and foremost have to be this:

> "If any man of the house of Israel or of the strangers that sojourn among them eats any blood, I will set my face against that person who

eats blood, and will cut him off from among his people. For the life of the flesh is in the blood; and I have given it for you upon the altar to make atonement for your souls; for it is the blood that makes atonement by reason of the life. Therefore I have said to the people of Israel, No person among you shall eat blood, neither shall any stranger who sojourns among you eat blood. Any man also of the people of Israel, or of the strangers that sojourn among them, who takes in hunting any beast or bird that may be eaten shall pour out its blood and cover it with dust. For the life of every creature is the blood of it; therefore I have said to the people of Israel, You shall not eat the blood of any creature, for the life of every creature is its blood; whoever eats it shall be cut off. (Leviticus 17:10-14)

Within Leviticus itself this ban is stated no less than four times – 3:17, 7:26-27, the above and 19:26a. In Deuteronomy we find it in 12:16, 12:23-25, 15:23, and again in I Samuel 14:32-34. You might think that, apart from the last instance, all this material comes from rather out-of-the-way places; but so deeply embedded was the ban in the Jewish mind that for first generation Christians (who were overwhelmingly converts from Judaism, and until Paul's time probably didn't even think of themselves as converts at all) it was still quite unthinkable that anyone should make light of it. We find it reaffirmed twice in Acts (15:29, 21:25) as one of the worst sins you could possibly commit. But it seems that Gentile converts were never really convinced by the ban; we find no mention of it elsewhere in the New Testament, nor in subsequent Christian literature. Nevertheless here is a practice whose specific condemnation in both Testaments is ignored by the Fundamentalist tradition.

The other claim to answer is that Fundamentalists believe the whole of the Bible to be literally true. As I said above, it will be immediately evident to any reasonably intelligent person reading the Bible that very little of it is literally true. What stand out above all as being simply not believable are the miracle stories, and particularly those of the gospels. This ought not to be at all a shocking thing to say because, if you think about it, we recognize a miracle story by virtue of the very fact that it can not be true; if the alleged event really could have happened, then we have no reason to regard it as miraculous. On the other hand, I do not think you could have a religion (I certainly couldn't have) without a miraculous element. As we shall see in the next chapter, one of the things we look for in religion is an unfailing hope of deliverance, and to be unfailing this hope has to be miraculous, because it is most valuable precisely in those situations where a purely rational estimate would offer no hope at all.

I would be the last person, therefore, to suggest that you can preach a gospel utterly purged of miraculous elements, but this is a very different thing from claiming that the miracles are literally true. How the miracle stories can be presented to 'unbelieving' hearers is too large a topic to be dealt with here; those who are interested in it will find a whole chapter devoted to the subject in my previous book on the Ten Commandments. The immediate point is that Fundamentalists will reply – with some justice – that what I am suggesting is far too subtle to be useful or helpful to the congregations they preach to. These are unsophisticated people (I in no way wish to sound scornful), most of whose time and energy is necessarily taken up with providing for themselves and their families, who do not have the time, even if they had the mental equipment, to pore over subtle distinctions between what is true and what is 'true'. I entirely accept that, and am happy with it; let them present the material in any way the auditory finds helpful.

Two things I would suggest, however. The first is that if you feel that your hearers cannot grasp the idea of a story that is 'true' but not true, then – rather than deliberately lie to them – do not discuss the question of its truth at all. I agree that the message loses all impact if you start by claiming that the story is not of course literally true; and that whatever you say subsequently, this will then be the only point that your hearers carry away with them, and that on its own it is scarcely a nourishing discourse. If you find a message of hope in the miracle stories, then go straight for that message, and do not bother your hearers with questions of whether the story is true or 'true'.

The other point is that, in contrast to Fundamentalist congregations, there are others which are sophisticated, who do not have to devote their whole energies to making provision, who do have the mental equipment (and find it very stimulating to use it) pondering distinctions between what is true and what is 'true', and the Fundamentalist tradition has no business getting in the way of such people or those who minister to them. It may seem unfair that some people have more leisure than others, more resources than others, more abilities than others, and perhaps indeed it is; but that is the world you have to work in, and experience tells us that it is a much poorer world without such differences. People who think about their religion and demand answers to their questions are not wicked, even if you can point to passages in Paul which suggest they are. They make difficulties for you only if you try to silence them; some of your own congregations may one day grow rich, or reflective, or both, or they may produce children showing such tendencies. In these circumstances you could find the subtleties of sophisticated believers very helpful to you.

I have rather wandered off the real point, which is much simpler than the above would suggest. Not only are the miracle stories not literally true, but (sad to say) most of the clergy who shout loudest that they are are themselves well aware that they are not. For them it is not a matter simply of believing them; you have *got* to believe them. And when anyone tells you that, it is a clear indication that the speaker himself in fact does not believe them. In the days when (just possibly) people really did believe the miracle stories, they wrote books about them (like the late C S Lewis) or conducted arguments about them in public to show that the stories, though miraculous, were still perfectly believable. But no one does that any longer, and from that we can reasonably conclude that, however much they protest to the contrary, modern Fundamentalist clergy do not in fact believe the miracle stories to be true at all.

We finish off with the biggest quandary of all, with the doctrine which is far and away the most important in the New Testament, and which Paul in particular undoubtedly accepted as literally true, but which the subsequent tradition has not been able to do since the end of the first century. And we begin with a text that, once again, has already been referred to:

> And he said to them, "Truly, I say to you, there are some standing here who will not taste death before they see the kingdom of God come with power." (Mark 9:1)

I have already made it clear from the evidence quoted previously that Paul himself believed this prediction to be literally true, and it is likely that all his contemporaries did the same. I have by no means given all the passages which make this clear, though I did refer to the most dramatic of them:

> I mean, brethren, the appointed time has grown very short; from now on, let those who have wives live as though they had none, and those who mourn as though they were not mourning, and those who rejoice as though they were not rejoicing, and those who buy as though they had no goods, and those who deal with the world as though they had no dealings with it. For the form of this world is passing away. (I Corinthians 7:29-31)

What makes this so startling is that Paul is not *primarily* concerned with the second coming here at all. He clearly thinks he is giving practical advice about everyday matters. "No need to bother about sex any more (or perhaps he means cleaning the house), or good luck, or bad luck, or buying or selling, or anything to do with the practical business of living in the world, because next week - or, at the very latest, next year - all that sort of thing will no longer have any relevance." And he clearly believed this literally; but how can any modern Fundamentalist claim to do the same? We can derive a "message" from it if we want to: "Paul means that, however immersed we may become in the business of this present world, we should remind ourselves that the day is not far off when we will be taken out of it, and all these things that seem so important now will no longer matter in the least. This will help to give us a sense of proportion." That is perfectly good, beneficial doctrine, but it is not the *literal* meaning of the above passage. The problem about that had already become acute before the latest document in the New Testament (II Peter) came to be written, and at one point the author of that text (not, of course, the apostle Peter) addresses himself to it:

> First of all you must understand this, that scoffers will come in the last days with scoffing, following their own passions and saying, "Where is the promise of his coming? For ever since the fathers fell asleep *[i.e. ever since the first generation Christians to whom the promise was made died off]*, all things have continued as they were from the beginning of creation." They deliberately ignore this one fact, that by the word of God heavens existed long ago, and an earth formed out of water and by means of water, through which the world that then existed was deluged with water and perished. But by the same word the heavens and earth that now exist have been stored up for fire, being kept until the day of judgment and destruction of ungodly men.
>
> But do not ignore this one fact, beloved, that with the Lord one day is as a thousand years, and a thousand years as one day. The Lord is not slow about his promises as some count slowness, but is forbearing toward you, not wishing that any should perish, but that all should reach repentance. But the day of the Lord will come like a thief, and then the heavens will pass away with a loud noise, and the elements will be dissolved with fire, and the earth and the works that are upon it will be burned up.

> Since all these things are thus to be dissolved, what sort of persons ought you to be in lives of holiness and godliness, waiting for and hastening the coming of the day of God, because of which the heavens will be kindled and dissolved, and the elements will melt with fire! But according to his promise we wait for new heavens and a new earth, in which righteousness dwells. (II Peter 3:3-13)

I have quoted this passage in its entirety because, although it contains a great deal that (I hope) not many people nowadays believe literally, it gives an overall impression of considerable beauty; and the final paragraph, though deriving from a whole string of fallacies, nevertheless manages to make a convincing point. But what I really want to draw attention to is the opening of the second paragraph: "But do not ignore this one fact, beloved, that with the Lord one day is as a thousand years, and a thousand years as one day". Fundamentalists tend to seize on this as vindicating the original prophecy, but if that is to count as a *literal* interpretation of the promise of "any day now", none of those rebuked by Fundamentalists for "explaining things away" need feel the least embarassment any longer. It would be hard to find a more blatant, contrived and dishonest *mis*interpretation of the perfectly plain – but mistaken – meaning of the original prophecy.

The Proper Use of Scripture

THE collection of books we know as the Old Testament seems to have had its origins in the trauma of the destruction of Jerusalem by the Babylonians in 586 BC. From the time of King David up to that event the nation seems to have identified itself above all with the monarchy, and then also with the city of Jerusalem and the royal cult in the Jerusalem temple. I suppose it could be argued we get an exaggerated idea of this in that Jeremiah, who is our best witness for the prevailing ideology of his time, himelf came from a priestly, and therefore in those days a fairly upper-class, family. But he could on occasion be critical of all these institutions while they still existed:

> This is the word which came to Jeremiah from the LORD, when King Zedekiah sent to him Pashhur the son of Malchiah and Zephaniah the priest, the son of Maaseiah, saying, " Inquire of the LORD for us, for Nebuchadrezzar king of Babylon is making war against us; perhaps the LORD will deal with us according to all his wonderful deeds, and will make him withdraw from us."
>
> Then Jeremiah said to them, "Thus you shall say to Zedekiah, 'Thus says the LORD, the God of Israel: Behold, I will turn back the weapons of war which are in your hands and with which you are fighting against the king of Babylon and against the Chaldeans who are besieging you outside the walls; and I will bring them together into the midst of this city. I myself will fight against you with outstretched hand and strong arm, in anger, and in fury, and in great wrath. And I will smite the inhabitants of this city, both man and beast; they shall die of a great pestilence. Afterward, says the LORD, I will give Zedekiah king of Judah, and his servants, and the people in this city who survive the pestilence, sword and famine, into the hand of Nebuchadrezzar king of Babylon and into the hand of their enemies, into the hand of those who seek their lives. He shall smite them with the edge of the sword; he shall

The Proper Use of Scripture

> not pity them, or spare them, or have compassion.'
>
> "And to this people you shall say: 'Thus says the LORD: Behold, I set before you the way of life and the way of death. He who stays in this city shall die by the sword, by famine and by pestilence; but he who goes out and surrenders to the Chaldeans who are besieging you shall live, and shall have his life as a prize of war. For I have set my face against this city for evil and not for good, says the LORD; it shall be given into the hand of the king of Babylon, and he shall burn it with fire. (Jeremiah 21:1-10)

It speaks volumes for the sacredness of the person of the prophet for Jeremiah's contemporaries that he should have uttered this kind of prophecy repeatedly during the very death agony of Jerusalem (there are a great many passages along the lines of the above throughout the book), and still have come out of it alive. The wonder is, not that the military men of the day tried to have him executed, but that he had enough influential friends to be able to prevent it.

Once the catastrophe has happened, though, Jeremiah completely changes his tune:

> The word of the LORD came to Jeremiah: "Thus says the LORD: If you can break my covenant with the day and my covenant with the night, so that day and night will not come at their appointed time, then also my covenant with David my servant may be broken, so that he shall not have a son to reign on his throne, and my covenant with the Levitical priests my ministers. As the host of heaven cannot be numbered and the sands of the sea cannot be measured, so I will multiply the descendants of David my servant, and the Levitical priests who minister to me." (Jeremiah 33:19-22)

There are many unfulfilled or erroneous prophecies throughout Scripture, but it would be hard to find one more absolute than this, and at the same time more absolutely wrong. At the time the prophecy was uttered the Levitical priests (i. e. the priests of the Jerusalem temple who, after the reforms of Josiah a generation earlier, were the the only ones still allowed to exercise a priestly function) still had six hundred years to go, before the final destruction of the Jerusalem temple in 70 AD consigned them to history. But the monarchy itself, although it is clear Jeremiah passionately hoped otherwise, had already gone for ever.

These were the beliefs that throughout the previous four hundred years had sustained the nation. First and foremost, the city was under God's direct protection and could never be captured. Israel seems to have inherited this idea from the city's earlier Canaanite inhabitants. When David was besieging the city in the eleventh century BC, the Canaanites taunted his army with the words:

> "You will not come in here, but the blind and the lame will ward you off" – thinking, "David cannot come in here." (II Samuel 5:6b)

Presumably Israel explained its own capture of Jerusalem as a ' proof' that God was on the side of Israel rather than of Canaan, and it seems to have held on to this dangerously complacent belief with enthusiasm. The whole of Psalm 48 is a celebration of it, and the events of II Kings 18: 13-29:37 (= Isaiah chapters 36 and 37) – though clearly distorted in the account we have, so that it is now very hard to make out what actually happened – only strengthened the delusion. The peculiar intensity we detect in the prophecies of Jeremiah (see particularly 7:1-20) are due to his perception that the idea was pure fantasy, and a fantasy that was leading the nation to its destruction.

When the city fell to the Babylonians, therefore, and was destroyed by them, it seemed to many that this was dramatic proof that the whole of this ideology was a sham. Jerusalem was no more sacred as a city that any other city, no more inviolable, no more indestructible. The monarchy had not after all been instituted by God, and the promises set out in II Samuel chapter 7, so far from being divinely made, were shown to be mere propaganda put out by David's court officials. It turned out after all that Israel was no different from all other nations, liable to the same fluctuations of good and bad fortune, of prosperity and disaster, of success in war and overthrow by it. Thus the world for Israel in 586 BC was a horrid, friendless and meaningless environment.

This was the situation which began the process of creating what we now call the Old Testament. The aim was to persuade the reader that the destruction of Jerusalem in 586 had no such implications as the 'realists' of the nation were insisting it had. Despite appearances to the contrary Jerusalem was indeed a sacred city, and would 'shortly' be rebuilt with even greater magnificence than it had showed at the time of its destruction; so would the temple, so would the priesthood, so would the law. The monarchy? There is little trace of a hope for its revival in the documents we have, but that is perhaps because it was not in fact revived, so that passages which bore witness to such a hope would have little interest for later scribes and would tend to be neglected. We can tell, nevertheless, that such hopes did in fact for a time centre on Zerubbabel the son of Shealtiel (see the prophecies of Haggai and chapters 1-8 of Zechariah).

A great deal of what survives in our Old Testament dates from before, and often long before, the destruction of Jerusalem; but the material which survives appears to be only quite a small selection of what was at one time available. The best illustration of this is the list of Solomon's 'writings' given in the first book of Kings:

> He also uttered three thousand proverbs; and his songs were a thousand and five. (I Kings 4:32)

Scholars tend to be derisive of the claim, but I find that hasty. I am not of course arguing that Solomon was indeed the author of the two collections that the author of I Kings is referring to, but I have no difficulty in accepting that he did know of a collection of three thousand proverbs, and another collection of a thousand and five songs, both of which were attributed to Solomon. Some of those proverbs may still be around in the extant book of Proverbs, and some *fragments* of those songs (for the whole of the Song of Songs is clearly a collection of fragments) may still survive in that book; but the losses as a whole have been enormous, and losses on the same scale have probably occurred in every branch of pre-Exilic literature.

What was selected for inclusion was chosen (and probably also edited and adapted) to give the impression that the catastrophe of 586 BC, so far from being the proof that God's promises were simply a fiction, was in fact an essential part of God's original plan in calling Israel to be his chosen instrument for setting up his rule on earth; that a new and chastened Israel would now take God's salvation to the very ends of the earth. The aim was to assert, in defiance of the evidence, that the destruction of Jerusalem was a confirmation, not a disproof, of the ideas that Israel had had of itself under the Davidic monarchy.

So the whole of the Bible is in fact a delusion? It can certainly be seen that way, and I have to admit that is how I myself tend to view it. In that case what possible value can it have? Isn't our present world built (and successfully built) upon reason? We tend to view delusions of this kind as always harmful, often dangerous, possibly insane. Yet I could point out that this hope, even if itself a delusion, has throughout history repeatedly brought about a deliverance that is absolutely real, and this could not be denied – though it could equally be said on the other side that the ideological hope of the Bible has a tendency to provoke the very disasters that it then enables its adherents to survive, and that also has truth in it.

My own reasons for identifying with the Bible have little to do with the course of history in general, but are largely personal. I first came across the Bible as a choirboy at the age of ten. Though I sang from the Psalter every day in the cathedral and heard the Old and New Testaments read to me, initially it was not this that made most impression on me. I had already undergone seven years of religious instruction at a Catholic convent school and, though I have no wish to criticize what I learnt there, what chiefly thrilled me in the new environment was having a Bible actually open before me, so that I no longer had to take what I was told on trust, but could turn the pages myself to see if that was what it really said. (Thus I well understand, even though I also somewhat deplore, the excitement of the Reformation age over the acquisition of a Bible it could read for itself, without having to rely on others to tell them what it said.)

It was after I left the choir school, and those daily dollops of Biblical indoctrination were no longer available, that I began to experience what I suppose would now be describe as withdrawal symptoms, in the form of bouts of depression that shaded off into less frequent, but much more distressing, panic attacks – as though the world really was round and I was falling off the edge of it. I began reading the Bible on my own account in the hope this might help keep me afloat – and it worked, quite literally as I thought at the time, 'miraculously'; the panic attacks disappeared altogether, and though the depressions did not (and did not for another thirty years) they worried me less, and I could live with them. At the time I believed this really was the work of God and he was saving me, and that this proved the truth of Christian claims, both about God himself and about the Bible. My subsequent experience has been that when you get to know the Bible well, you can see how this effect is achieved, and that there is nothing miraculous about it; but I've never been able to see how such a realization can be thought to 'disprove' the Bible. I still read from it twice daily, and I get the same kind of benefit from doing so as I always have, even if my understanding of what these benefits are has changed utterly.

I tell you all this because it has helped me to see that though the Bible does indeed falsify experience, it is precisely by doing so that it offers the hope of redemption. When I went up to Oxford to read theology, it was generally held that the Bible offered the possibility of knowing the truth about God's purposes for man, but that this truth lay hidden under a heavy layer of distortion; and that the task of the expositor was to strip away the distortion to reveal the underlying truth. This notion, as I shall demonstrate below, has been disastrous. There is an underlying historical truth, and we can often come close to seeing what it is; but if we make that the end of our endeavours, we are left with knowledge that is true but entirely trivial. The purpose of revealing this historic truth is that we can then see how, in the Biblical account of it, it has been distorted, and why it has; and it is the *distortion* that tells us what the message is. This message lies, not in the original event which, of itself, has little meaning, but in the way the Biblical account refashions it.

By way of a slight digression, I said above that aim of criticism, as it was understood when I was young and still is by more than a few of the academically-minded, has had disastrous consequences for religion as a whole. What I had in mind was the constant upheavals, particularly in the matter of the liturgy, that all churches have been subject to in the last thirty to forty years. The aim here too has been to strip away the ' cultural baggage that has accumulated over the centuries' to reveal the 'essential underlying message'. It is as though we encountered a magnificent marble tomb and decided that we must dismantle it to reveal the paltry remains that it concealed. What has gone is what was valued, and it is hard to see that what is left has any real value at all. We are left, not with the 'underlying reality', but with a gaping hole, a scattering of dust and a few mouldering bones.

On the other hand, how do we justify 'belief' in what we know is not the truth? But that is in fact quite easy to do. Look at experience generally. The historian will tell us that to think of history as having any kind of meaning or purpose is always an obstacle in the way of giving an honest and convincing account of the evidence before him. In the same way the scientist will tell us that to think of the world around us as having meaning or purpose gets in the way of arriving at an understanding of how it actually works; and in his case he can point to his undoubted ability to manipulate that world to our advantage as proof that his understanding of it is superior, for instance, to that of a pious or religious admiration. But when we come to look at our own selves, the position is reversed: 'reason' here, just as much as in history or science, will tell us that we have no real significance, that our lives have no real meaning or purpose, that it is a matter of indifference to nature, history and the universe at large whether we prosper or decay, whether we overcome or are vanquished, whether we live or die. And there are lots of people around who are very conscious of the truth of all this. But if we want to find them, where do we look? Among the powerful? Among the wealthy? Among the honoured? Among the revered? No, we'll usually find them either sleeping rough or in the mad house.

If we evaluate ourselves solely in terms of reason, the most sensible course of action indicated at every moment in our lives is suicide. We live and are happy and are prosperous only if we can manage to maintain the most preposterous delusions about ourselves: that we ourselves matter, that our lives have a meaning and a purpose, and that the world around us is actually meant to serve that purpose. I myself am particularly conscious of this because I was well into my thirties before I ever managed to feel that way, and until I did so I felt more or less permanently bewildered. If we find there is a high suicide rate among people who have been brought up in care, the likeliest reason is not that they have been sexually abused (though they may have been), but that they have never learnt to feel this way about themselves. (There is also the point, though, that they come out into the world without money, possessions, friends, resources, usually without qualifications and without a place to stay, and after a year or two of struggling desperately and getting nowhere they conclude they would be better off dead; and, sadly, they are usually right about that.) It looks as though, if we have a normal childhood, we acquire these delusions naturally, so that we are not even aware of them; the only people likely to realize the need for them are those that have not in fact acquired them.

What a successful family background does for the individual it is the task of religion to do for society as a whole; to replace a dispiriting realism, which simply undermines self-confidence, with a delusive – but also apparently redemptive – fiction that we *do* matter, that as a group we have an identity which is 'real', that our communal aims are authenticated by a higher power than our earthly selves. It also helps the individual this way, as I know from my own experience; but it is essential for the stability and cohesion of the community, and the political order in all societies until modern times has always recognized this.

Why then, for the present century, does all this no longer seem to be so? Once again the likeliest answer is easily discerned. It is the case with all of us that we long to feel we are living in a world which we can feel is on our side, and most of the time we find this illusion difficult to maintain. Religion aims to convince us – yes, in defiance of the evidence – that in fact we do. It makes no change to any part of our experience; it simply reinterprets that experience in a way that makes it now seem friendly and benign. But over the last two or three hundred years we think we have found a better way. Strip away the illusions, we tell ourselves, examine the world around us as it really is, and we find we can actually change it in ways that really do render it benign and an our side. When I was young it was genuinely believed that, given time, all problems could be solved by scientific advance and, if not ourselves, then our children or the generation after them would be living, if not actually in a perfect world, then one whose imperfections could be quickly understood and quickly remedied. Not many people think this now (though there are some). The big miscalculation in that blue-print was that we had not yet grasped that the resources of the planet we live on are finite; that we are locked into a system which can only function by growing, and that clearly we cannot hope that it will carry on growing for ever; and we deeply fear that when the growing has to stop we shall all be faced with an unimaginable calamity.

This has been a lengthy digression but I hope it has made clear that it is in fact quite easy to defend 'belief' in ideas that we perfectly well realize are illusory. That is really what 'faith' is, though I would be reluctant to conclude from that that everything calling itself 'faith' is thereby justified. How then do we recognize a faith that is justified? We don't, we have to choose one – and the point must also be made that we don't necessarily choose it for ourselves; it is perfectly right and proper that the choice should be made for us, by the family into which we are born, by the community to which we belong, by the nation at large. If we insist on individual choice, there are two big disadvantages that follow: the first is that a large and in the event very troublesome section of the community will choose nothing much at all; and secondly, if we all make our own individual choice, the likeliest consequence is the general dissolution of community rather than stability and cohesion.

The Bible, then, offers a message of hope, even if we may often feel it is an illusory hope; (but as I said earlier, the choice before us is not between a real hope and an illusory hope, but between an illusory hope and no hope at all). And it is this message of hope, and not the rules and regulations, which is the real purpose of having a Bible; and whatever deprives men of this hope negates the real purpose of the Bible, however much the negation itself may be couched in Biblical terms. Perhaps there really are some people who, through no fault of their own, are excluded from the message of hope which the Bible offers. I would hate to think so, but it cannot be denied that Calvin was right in suggesting that the Bible itself occasionally makes something like that suggestion:

> . . . when Rebecca had conceived children by one man, our forefather Isaac, though they were not yet born and had done nothing either good or bad, in order that God's purpose of election might continue, not because of works but because of his call *[i.e. not because of our own efforts to be virtuous - which cannot succeed - but because of God's*

offering us salvation regardless of our efforts], she was told, "The elder will serve the younger". As it is written, "Jacob I loved, but Esau I hated". (Romans 9:10-13)

There undoubtedly are people who come into this world in circumstances – or with a heredity – so unfortunate, whose character or appearance as a result of this is so unprepossessing, that we may be tempted to feel that all real hope has been denied them at birth, and through no fault of their own. I would hate to think this is so, but I confess I lack the confidence to insist that it certainly never can be so. But homosexuality is not an affliction of this kind, and there is no reason why it should be an affliction of any kind. Plenty of societies in every age have managed to accommodate it, and where it does cause problems it will usually be found on examination that the problems are caused not by homosexuality itself but by the dogmatic and unreasonable condemnation of it. Despite all protest to the contrary it is a natural condition; by that I mean that it is not the result of choice, or corruption, or sinfulness, or any kind of deliberate perversity, but that it is found to occur naturally in all herd or social animals. Those societies which have acknowledged it and established legitimate channels for its expression have on the whole been culturally richer, more at ease with themselves, more calmly rational than those which have thought it necessary to prohibit it, to condemn it, or to punish it.

Undoubtedly we do need rules (though I suspect that Jesus himself might well have had severe doubts about that), and undoubtedly the Bible does have a direct connection with the rules we need. But the Bible cannot simply be used as a rule book; it can advise us on the kind of rules we need, but it cannot supply them. No one of any sense will be surprised to be told that the rules which worked well in 1,400 BC are not the same as those we need in 2,000 AD. The Bible unquestionably condemns homosexuality in both Old and New Testaments, but it condemns the eating of black pudding even more vehemently. Obedience may well be a virtue, but it is by no means the same as virtue, and blind obedience is not a virtue at all. Blind obedience is the vice of those who would rather not have to think about virtue in the first place.